Pauline Kinney
From
Audry Swartz

RUTH

A Life of Love and Loyalty

RUTH
A Life of Love and Loyalty

by
CHARLES E. FULLER

FLEMING H. REVELL COMPANY

To my loving wife, Grace Payton Fuller, whose prayers, counsel, and devotion on our wilderness journey have lightened the trials and furthered the success of the Old Fashioned Revival Hour.

Foreword

As OUR LORD turned the water into wine at the marriage feast in Cana, so He has been pleased to use these simple expositions of the Book of Ruth to quicken many from death unto life and to edify the saints in their most holy faith. In response to numerous requests, we have felt led to commit them to writing with the hope and prayer that the Spirit of God, who blessed the spoken word, may now endue the written word with the same power and grace, that all they who read may have the eyes of their minds enlightened and their wills renewed to embrace Jesus Christ, God's Kinsman-Redeemer, as their personal Saviour.

CHARLES E. FULLER
San Marino, California

Contents

Contents

RUTH
A Life of Love and Loyalty

I

A Famine in the Land

Now it came to pass in the days when the judges ruled, that there was a famine in the land. And a certain man of Bethlehem-judah went to sojourn in the country of Moab, he, and his wife, and his two sons. (Ruth 1:1)

Ruth is one of the greatest love stories of all time. Judged merely as an inspiring piece of literature, the book will echo through the ages. Ruth is the Cinderella of the Scriptures, and her life is a model of dignity and unshaken devotion to those things which are highest and noblest in life. Here in four short chapters a lowly maid from the land of Moab becomes the wife of a wealthy land-owner, Boaz, who lived in Bethlehem several centuries before this little village was immortalized by the birth of our Saviour. The reality of love as a great power in life is displayed as we see the hearts of Naomi, Ruth and Boaz joined and knit together by its inviolable bonds. This book is a beautiful commentary on the words of the Apostle Paul: "And now abideth faith, hope, love, these three; but the greatest of these is love" (I Corinthians 13:13).

But the primary reason why we should acquaint ourselves with this little book is not for its literary appeal, but because it is a part of God's inspired Word. There are many lessons which the Spirit of God will teach the devout student of Ruth, if he will submit his mind to the wisdom and the truth which it contains.

BACKGROUND OF THE STORY

By way of background we should remember that the covenant promise which God made with Abraham, the father of the Jewish race, included, among other things, the assurance that in Abraham would all nations of the earth be blessed. Now in the story of Ruth we see how this is so. A Gentile girl marries an Israelite, a prominent Jewish landowner, and in so doing turns her back upon the gods of her people and embraces the one true and living God, who had revealed Himself to the Jewish people of old. If we would know what salvation means, we must do what Ruth did. We must become sons of Abraham by faith in our Lord Jesus Christ, in order that we may be heirs of the promise made to Abraham and to his seed. Let us bear this ever in mind as we study this book.

Another interesting fact by way of background and introduction is that the orthodox Israelite of today, when he celebrates the feast of Pentecost or harvest time, reads the Book of Ruth. This feast is in the fall of the year when the crops are gathered in, and you will notice throughout the Book of Ruth many references to the gleaning of wheat at the time of the harvest. In fact, it is in the field of Boaz, where she is gleaning after the reapers, that Ruth first meets the man who is destined to become her benefactor and her husband. In the language of the Old Testament, Boaz is called her kinsman-redeemer. In like manner Christ is our Kinsman-Redeemer. Thus Boaz is a type of our Lord and Saviour, Jesus Christ. Let us remember these truths as we approach the study of the text, beginning with the first verse of the book: "Now it came to pass in the days when the judges ruled, that there was a famine in the land."

THE DAYS WHEN THE JUDGES RULED

First, a brief word about the phrase, "Now it came to pass." This grouping of words occurs six times in the Word of God and in each occurrence denotes some impending trouble, followed by a happy deliverance. As the story in the Book of Ruth unfolds, we will see that this is the message of the book—a story of trouble and of judgment, followed by the gracious moving of God in order to deliver those who put their faith and trust in Him. The setting for this time of trouble and deliverance is "the days when the judges ruled." If you are at all acquainted with the Book of Judges, which is one of the most neglected and yet important books in the Old Testament, you realize that these were evil days religiously and morally in ancient Israel. Constantly the people turned aside unto the gods of the Canaanites, the false gods which they were supposed to have uprooted and driven from the land. And as a result of this religious apostasy, the moral standards of the day disintegrated, until we find again and again the statement that "Every man did that which was right in his own eyes." Now as a result of this apostasy and moral decadence, God visited His people with judgment. The text goes on to say that "there was a famine in the land." If any of you have ever had the experience of living under drought conditions, you may have some appreciation of the suffering that such circumstances bring. Here we have the story of a family broken up by this judgment of God. The land is becoming parched and unfruitful, the sheep are dying on the bare hillsides, the cattle languish in the fields, and from the usually fertile soil little corn is being reaped.

ELIMELECH'S DISOBEDIENCE

Elimelech sees his possessions melting away and decides that until the famine is over he must seek refuge in the well-watered fields of Moab on the other side of the Dead Sea. It was not very far and he probably thought to himself that he would return and resume his accustomed life in his old home and with his own people as soon as the crisis had passed. For you and me such a decision could never have all the implications that it had for a devout Jew. If we decide for various reasons to leave our homeland and live in another land, there are family ties that will be broken; there are many political and economic factors that will have to be considered. But for the Israelite in Old Testament times, there was a religious question involved. The land in which he lived was part of the covenant blessing which he had inherited from his father Abraham, and God was especially to be worshiped in the tabernacle where He dwelt in the midst of His people in the land. Therefore, for an Israelite to leave the land was not simply a matter of emigration, but something which he did with risk and peril to his soul's well-being. This was a great decision which Elimelech had to make.

Elimelech means "My God is King," and, as this name implies, we may suppose that he was one who worshiped the God of Israel. Undoubtedly, as we have said, he had no thought or intention of forsaking the God of his fathers when he left the land, but the real proof of a man's faith is how he reacts when he is put under trial. We see the true heart and character of a man when he is under severe testing. Such was the situation with Elimelech. From the natural standpoint matters appeared quite hopeless, and no doubt Elimelech began to be tempted to ask, "Is God really

King? Can God supply my every need, especially in the face of such a crisis as this?" Perhaps you have been tempted with the same thoughts. Perhaps your troubles seem more than you can bear and you have begun to doubt God, and doubt His love and His providential care for you. But remember, God's Word says: "There hath no temptation taken you but such as is common to man: but God is faithful, who will not suffer you to be tempted above that ye are able; but will with the temptation also make a way to escape, that ye may be able to bear it" (I Corinthians 10:13).

Now as we watch Elimelech, we cannot but be disappointed in what he did. Unbelief crept into his heart and, as a result, he was found in the way of disobedience. He left the land of his citizenship to go and sojourn in the land of heathen idolaters. By his actions Elimelech was saying in effect: "God is not my King; God cannot supply my every need, His grace is not sufficient for me." We might say of Elimelech, as we must say of so many today, that, though he had the form of godliness, yet he lacked the power thereof. Though he seemed to be alive, yet he really was dead spiritually. He was not spiritually-minded, but carnally-minded, and after the second chapter of the book he drops from the picture. He is never again mentioned, either in the Book of Ruth or in the entire Scripture. You will notice that he has no place in the Westminster Abbey of faith in the eleventh chapter of Hebrews. He made his choice and the last we hear of him is that he died in the land of Moab.

WHERE IS YOUR CITIZENSHIP?

Are you spiritually-minded, or are you carnally-minded? The Scriptures say that to be carnally-minded is death, and that if you willfully sin against God and turn your back on Him and associate with those who are of this world, who worship other gods, the time will come when God will say to you, "I give you up." There is a sin unto death, John tells us, and he says that we should not even pray for those who have committed this sin. God forbid that any who are reading these words should be guilty of this sin. The Lord has made a way of escape through Jesus Christ, who shed His precious blood on Calvary's cross in order that we might be cleansed from all our sin. Will you not come in humility and confession, saying, "Oh Lord, be merciful to me, a sinner, and save me for

Christ's sake"? Remember Jesus says, ". . . him that cometh to me I will in no wise cast out" (John 6:37).

Do not, like Elimelech, turn your back upon God and seek to save yourself. Do not compromise with the world. No doubt Elimelech reasoned that the people of Moab spoke a language very similar to Hebrew; they were husbandmen and herdsmen like the Hebrews, and he thought that he would find in the fields of Moab a place to live that was very much like home and far more comfortable and safe. But the truth of the matter is that in Moab the people worshiped the false god, Chemosh, and the worship of this god involved rites and festivals which were a disgrace to humanity and a degradation of the worship which is due to the only one true and living God. Eventually Elimelech settled down there in Moab and his sons married daughters from the land, and he never did return to the land of promise and to the God of his fathers. And so it may be with you. If you choose to live in this world as a citizen of this world and turn your back on God, you will never attain to that better land and that better life. I therefore beseech you to seek the Lord that ye may find Him and be saved.

II

God's Dealings with Naomi

And Elimelech Naomi's husband died; and she was left, and her two sons. And they took them wives of the women of Moab; the name of the one was Orpah, and the name of the other Ruth: and they dwelt there about ten years. And Mahlon and Chilion died also both of them; and the woman was left of her two sons and her husband.

Then she arose with her daughters in law, that she might return from the country of Moab: for she had heard in the country of Moab how that the Lord had visited his people in giving them bread. Wherefore she went forth out of the place where she was, and her two daughters in law with her; and they went on the way to return unto the land of Judah. And Naomi said unto her two daughters in law, Go, return each to her mother's house: the Lord deal kindly with you, as ye have dealt with the dead, and with me. (Ruth 1:3–8)

The Word of God is like a great looking glass. As we see the Lord dealing in other ages with men and women of like passions with ourselves, we gain a deeper understanding of our own spiritual experience and learn how we should walk before Him who is our Maker and our Redeemer.

Now the events in the Book of Ruth occurred over a period of about ten years, back in the days when the judges ruled in Israel. As we have said, those were desperate days, days of disobedience, of dark counsel and lawless apostasy, days when men did not take God into their thoughts, but did only that which was right in their own eyes. And God visited His people with judgment. He chastened them with a great famine for their disobedience and waywardness. This scene of judgment is the setting for the tragic and beautiful story of Ruth. In our first meditation, we had occasion to mention the beginnings of the tragedy in the home of Elimelech and Naomi, and to reflect upon the sad choice which they made under the duress of circumstance: the decision to take their children and go into a strange land where the true God was not worshiped and where His name was not known.

GOD'S CHASTISEMENT

Today we shall see how the hand of God was upon them, chastising them for their sins. (Let us take warning, that we fall not after the same example of disobedience.) First of all, Elimelech died and Naomi was left with her two sons. As we can tell from what happens later on in the book, Naomi was a true, godly woman. It may be that she did not wish to do as her husband did. Perhaps she remonstrated with Elimelech, pleaded with him that God would supply their needs in Bethlehem and take care of them even in the midst of famine, according to His promise. But, being an obedient wife, and realizing that Elimelech was the head of the home, she submitted to him quietly and went with him, taking her two sons. If this was the case, Elimelech surely ought to have listened to his godly wife and paid heed to her wise word of counsel. The Scriptures say that a good wife is an exceedingly precious treasure and a man should be thankful to God if he is blessed with such an helpmeet. But Elimelech, like Demas, loved this present world. Therefore, he did not heed sound admonition, but turned his back on God and went to live in a land where he hoped he might prosper in the things of this life. He did not trust the Lord to take care of him.

But, to continue our story, we see how God chastened Naomi with the rod of His correction in order that He might bring her back into a loving fellowship with Himself. The Scripture says, "For whom the Lord loveth he chasteneth, and scourgeth every son whom he receiveth" (Hebrews 12:6). Now there are no exceptions to this rule and oftentimes some of the severest chastisements are experienced by those whom God loves most dearly, just because He does love them so much and wishes to make them His obedient children.

NAOMI'S SEVERE TRIAL

Let us see now how Naomi reacts under severe testing and trial. The first great stroke of the rod of correction in her life was the loss of her husband. We read, "And Elimelech Naomi's husband died; and she was left, and her two sons." Elimelech lost his life while seeking a livelihood, and the land which he had sought to be his home became his grave. Apparently death overtook him rather suddenly and not long after he had come to the land of Moab. Though it is appointed unto men once to die, yet death is the one thing men never take into their plans.

After their father's death, we read that the two sons of Naomi took wives of the women of Moab. The name of the one was Orpah and the other Ruth. This, no doubt, was also a burden to Naomi, a godly Israelite, for she could not but have thought upon the prohibition in Deuteronomy 7:2–4: ". . . thou shalt make no covenant with them . . . Neither shalt thou make marriages with them; thy daughter thou shalt not give unto his son, nor his daughter shalt thou take unto thy son. For they will turn away thy son from following me, that they may serve other gods. . . ." Just as the land was part of the covenant made with Abraham, so marriage to those who were of the godly race was also a part of that covenant, and even in the New Testament we find that the Apostle Paul admonishes Christians that they should marry only in the Lord (II Corinthians 6:14–18). Marriage, of course, is a very intimate and close fellowship, and if we marry those who do not share our faith and do not love and serve our Saviour, then we reveal that we do not love Him most of all.

The Apostle Paul asks, ". . . what communion hath

light with darkness? And what concord hath Christ with Belial?" (vs. 14–15). Perhaps Naomi had wanted to leave Moab upon the death of Elimelech, but her two sons were determined to settle down in the land. Like their father, they wanted their own way. They would pay no attention to the law of God. It would appear from some of the things which are said in the Old Testament that the daughters of Moab were especially obnoxious to the devout Israelites. They were a fascinating, wanton, profligate race of women. They practiced human sacrifice and would cast their own children into the burning arms of the sacrificial flames. It was, no doubt, a great mercy on God's part that He spared Mahlon and Chilion from such women. They seemed to have made an exceptionally fortunate choice in those whom they took to be their wives. Though we know that they never turned their wives to the service of the true God, yet it does not appear that their wives turned them to their false gods. (Later on Ruth determined to take her shelter under the wing of the God of Israel, but Orpah, we are expressly told, went back to her people and to her gods.)

Finally, the most crushing blow of all was to fall

upon Naomi's head. Both of her sons died there in the land of Moab. And now she was bereft of her husband and of her children. She was utterly destitute; but man's extremity is the Lord's opportunity. Though He chastens His children with a rod, He will not cast them off forever. Though He cause them grief, yet He puts their tears in His bottle and has compassion upon them according to the multitude of His mercy, for He does not willingly afflict the children of men. Therefore, we should learn not to distrust the love of God in affliction, as Naomi did, but rather to look upon it as the chastening of the Lord and purpose in our hearts to return to His fellowship and to His people. For if, when we transgress, we confess our sins, we will find that He is always faithful and just to forgive us our sins and to cleanse us from all unrighteousness.

HEAR THE VOICE OF THE LORD

Notice verse 6: "Then [that is, after the death of her sons] she arose . . . that she might return from the country of Moab. . . ." Her life turned to ashes in Moab, but now she will seek the beauty which the Lord alone can give. Has God been speaking to you through adverse circumstances? Has God been chastening you because of your waywardness, because of your lack of fellowship? Will you not then learn a lesson from Naomi and resolve in your heart to return unto the Lord and to seek His face, knowing that with the Lord there is plenteous mercy and that He will abundantly pardon? Turn to your Bible and read Jeremiah 3:12, 13: ". . . Return, thou backsliding Israel, saith the Lord; and I will not cause mine anger to fall upon you: for I am merciful . . . I will not keep anger for ever. Only acknowledge thine iniquity, that thou hast transgressed against the Lord thy God . . . and ye have not obeyed my voice. . . ." Will you today acknowledge your sins? Will you own your transgressions and pour out your heart in confession to the one and only Mediator and High Priest, the Lord Jesus Christ? For the Lord says, Return and I will heal your backslidings.

GOD'S MERCY IN TRIBULATION

The text says that Naomi heard in the land of Moab how the Lord had visited His people in giving them bread. Wherefore she went forth from the place where she was with her two daughters-in-law. Evidently, although there had been much sorrow in the home, there had been some measure of happiness and fellowship between Naomi and these two girls, for she said, ". . . The Lord deal kindly with you, as ye have dealt with the dead, and with me. The Lord grant you that ye may find rest, each of you in the house of her husband" (Ruth 1:8, 9). Then she kissed them and they lifted up their voices and wept. Never is there anything in this life so bitter but that there is some sweet with it. Never is there a tragedy but that there is also mercy. Never does God so forsake His people but what He leaves some tokens of His fatherly kindness. And so it was here. Though the mother had, no doubt, looked upon the decision of her sons to take foreign women for their wives with some misgiving and though these wives were not worshipers of the true God, yet they were kindly disposed to their mother-in-law and their hearts seem to have been knit to hers by the common sorrow and tragedy which had overtaken them.

Under these circumstances, it may seem to us strange advice to come from a godly woman that she urged Ruth and Orpah to return to the land of Moab. But we must remember that she was a destitute old woman who could guarantee them no security if they were to leave the land and the people amongst whom they had lived. We may gather from the free way in which Naomi speaks about the Lord that she had taught them something of the true faith; she now commits them to His keeping and to His care that He may give them rest and a measure of happiness, but she does not feel that she is in any position to urge upon them to take the risk of leaving all and coming with her. The times were rude and wild and a woman could be safe and respected only under the protection of a husband. These women of antiquity were not like many of our career women today. They could not conceive of life in any other way than arranged around the family with the man as the head of the home. And how could Ruth and Orpah find favor in Bethlehem? Their speech, their manners, and all their background would be despised and rejected. They had no property, they had no dowry; and apparently Naomi, who had learned so much from the bitter exile that she had endured from her own native land, did not wish to bring life's sufferings upon her daughters-in-law in a strange land.

THE TRIUMPH OF FAITH

Now, in the midst of this dramatic scene of parting and farewell, Ruth gives evidence of a beautiful and unshakeable faith. In spite of all the hazards and all the difficulties, all the seeming impossibilities, she is determined to go with her mother-in-law and to be numbered amongst the people of the God of Israel. This is the kind of faith that saves, that brings one into fellowship with God. Do you have that kind of faith? Are you willing to risk all, whatever it may cost, in order to have the God of Israel as your God? Jesus tells us that if we would be His disciples we must take up our cross daily and follow Him. It is not easy to be a Christian. It cost Ruth everything to leave the security of her native land and venture forth by faith into a strange land and among strange people, but she did not waver. Unlike her sister, who turned back to her gods, Ruth chose to worship the God of Israel and thus she passed from death unto life. Do you have the witness in your heart of such an experience as this? The Lord says, "Him that cometh to me I will in no wise cast out" (John 6:37). He did not cast Ruth out as we shall see; and if you will come as did she, He will not cast you out either, but will accept you and will do for you more than you could ever ask or think. Will you not come today?

III

Ruth Clave unto Her

*And they lifted up their voice, and wept again: and Orpah
kissed her mother in law; but Ruth clave unto her. And
she said, Behold, thy sister in law is gone back unto her
people, and unto her gods: return thou after thy sister in
law. And Ruth said, Intreat me not to leave thee, or to
return from following after thee: for whither thou goest,
I will go; and where thou lodgest, I will lodge: thy people
shall be my people, and thy God my God: Where thou
diest, will I die, and there will I be buried: the Lord do
so to me, and more also, if aught but death part thee and
me. (Ruth 1:14–17)*

Here we have a most dramatic and moving scene:
three widows at the crossroads of moral decision. May
the Holy Spirit enlighten the eyes of our understand-

ing in a most unusual way as we consider this important moment in the lives of Naomi and her daughters-in-law, for we, as they, stand at the same crossroads. As they, we must choose what God we shall serve.

TWO FATEFUL DECISIONS

These things, like all other things in the Scripture, are for our example, written for our admonition and our instruction in the paths of righteousness. As we have already had occasion to observe, evidently Naomi, by her life and testimony, had taught her daughters-in-law concerning the true God of Israel, and there had grown up between them strong ties of mutual affection and esteem. So much was this so that now that she is about to leave and return to her native land, the two girls take it more or less as a matter of course that they will return with her. But when the fateful hour to depart comes, Naomi disabuses their minds of any false sense of security or any lack of understanding of the great implications that such a choice would carry with it. She tells them frankly that they would do far better to return to the homes of their respective mothers for she has nothing that she can give them and they face the prospect of loneliness and of suffering in an unknown land if they go with her. At this point an amazing difference between these two young women is brought to the surface, a difference, in all likelihood, which Naomi herself did not fully realize before. Orpah contemplates the picture of her future as Naomi paints it. She sees indeed that it would be much safer for her to return to her native home. The possibilities of humiliation, the dangers and the uncertainties of the course before her finally prevail upon her mind and she gives her mother-in-law a fateful kiss, turns and, weeping as she goes, walks slowly back from whence she had come. Undoubtedly she often looked back while her friends were yet in sight and watched them as slowly, step by step, they passed out of her sight and out of her life into a new existence which she was never to know.

And now comes Ruth's supreme moment. She has not only the advice of her mother-in-law with which to struggle, but also the example of her sister-in-law. Will she too turn back? Never! Nothing deters her. She cleaves unto Naomi and answers her in the famous and moving passage, which is a model of unshakeable devotion, concluding with the words, "the Lord do so to me, and more also, if aught but death part thee and me." Thus Ruth forever silences any doubts which may have assailed her mind and resolves to act upon the great truth that the God of Naomi, the God of Abraham, Isaac and Jacob, shall certainly be her God. You who have heard the way of salvation, you are now put before the same choice which faced Ruth of old on the borders of Moab and Judah. What will be your decision? Will you go back and serve the gods of this present evil world, or will you press on and declare yourself to be a member of the household of faith, number yourself with the people of God, enter into the blessing of everlasting life, of heaven and home? This decision means the difference between heaven and hell. Your soul's eternal destiny may hang, and does hang, on the narrow thread of a moment in time—the moment of your decision for or against the truth, for or against Jesus Christ, the only Saviour and Redeemer of God's people.

THE COST OF DISCIPLESHIP

We read in the New Testament in Matthew 8:19, 20 how a certain scribe came unto our Lord and said unto Him, "Master, I will follow thee whithersoever thou goest." But Jesus said unto him, "The foxes have holes, and the birds of the air have nests; but the Son of man hath not where to lay his head." Jesus knew the cost of discipleship. He said that if we would follow Him, we must forsake all, otherwise we cannot be His disciples. We must put Christ first. Our own possessions, our own business, our own prosperity, our very lives must all be secondary. Christ must have the pre-eminence.

Undoubtedly Orpah had a kind of faith in the God of Naomi, for surely she had heard of Him. She had a head knowledge, but not a heart experience; she had an outward *form* of godliness, but in the moment of supreme testing, she did not have the *power* of godliness. The Scripture speaks of the offense of the cross. It speaks of those in Hebrews 6:4-6 who have once been enlightened, who have tasted of the heavenly gift and been made partakers of the Holy Ghost, who have known something of the powers of the world to come, and then fall away. And it has this solemn warning that if we fall away, it is impossible again to renew us unto repentance, seeing we crucify to ourselves the Son of God afresh and put Him to an open

39

shame. Those of you who have heard the gospel are placed before a tremendous responsibility. You have been told how Christ died for your sins, how He was buried and rose again on the third day. If you turn your back on Him and choose the things of this world and of this life, you crucify Him afresh.

Orpah was like those who receive the Word with gladness, but it took no root in her heart. Springing up for a little season, it flourished, but under the hot sun of testing, it withered away and died. What a contrast with her sister-in-law, Ruth. Naomi said, "Behold, thy sister in law is gone back unto her people, and unto her gods: return thou after thy sister in law" (Ruth 1:15). But Ruth replies with such a fervor of conviction that from this moment on and throughout the remainder of the book, she charms us with the beauty of her character and becomes more dear to us perhaps than any other woman in the Old Testament. God made the path of duty straight and plain before her face and she resolved that she would walk in it, come what may. Will you follow in her footsteps today? You cannot escape the necessity of a personal decision. You cannot drift into salvation along with your friends, your family and your church.

CHRIST, OUR MOST PRECIOUS POSSESSION

What a remarkable change comes over Ruth; a change which can only be called conversion. She renounces the gods of her fathers. She chooses the God of Israel. Like the disciples whom Jesus called, who left their father and their fishing nets and all that they had and straightway followed Him, she gives up everything that she had known and which had been dear to her. She leaves all behind for the sake of her new-found faith. Paul said, ". . . I count all things but loss for the excellency of the knowledge of Christ Jesus my Lord . . ." (Philippians 3:8). It is written again of Moses: "By faith . . . when he was come to years, [he] refused to be called the son of Pharaoh's daughter; Choosing rather to suffer affliction with the people of God, than to enjoy the pleasures of sin for a season; Esteeming the reproach of Christ greater riches than the treasures in Egypt: for he had respect unto the recompence of the reward" (Hebrews 11:24–26). God needs men and women of courage who will stand this day and be numbered on His side, who are willing to renounce the pleasures of the world with all its alluring treasure for His sake. I love that song,

"Take the world, but give me Jesus." I urge upon you once more to consider this all-demanding question of our Lord, "For what shall it profit a man, if he shall gain the whole world, and lose his own soul?" (Mark 8:36). You who are young and desire an education, what will you do with your knowledge if your mind is not enlightened with the wisdom from on high? You who are rich and have silver and gold and lands and possessions, what will it profit you if you are not reconciled to God, if you die in your sins, if you spend eternity without God and without hope? Is Jesus really dwelling in your heart, by faith, or are you like Orpah? You know the truth but you do not act upon it. You go through the form and ceremonies, but there is no power, no depth, no life in it all. There are many people who suppose that if they commit themselves to Christ they will have to give up too much, but actually they are only giving up ashes for beauty, rags for the robes of Christ's righteousness.

GOD'S ABUNDANT BLESSINGS

When Ruth, on the banks of the Jordan, turned her back forever upon the land of Moab and started up the steep, narrow ascent through the Judean hills,

little did she know what God had in store for her.
But, as the story unfolds, we shall see her faith increased; and with her increased faith, she moved into
a fulfillment of her life in realizing the highest joy and
privilege that womankind can know. She became the
mother of a son from whose loins came David the
King, and eventually Jesus, the Messiah, our Lord and
Saviour. And thus the lines fell to her in pleasant
places and God showed Himself benevolent, kind and
merciful to her beyond anything that she could have
hoped or dreamed. And so it will be with you, if you,
like Ruth, will come to Him. He will do for you exceedingly abundantly above all that you ask or think.
He will pardon all your sins and He will clothe you
with the righteousness of Christ and make you a new
creature in Him. If God is speaking to you today, if
the Holy Spirit strives with you, I cannot urge you
too earnestly, like Ruth, to make your decision now
while it is today. Let nothing deter you. See how
Ruth, by faith, meets every disuasive plea of her
mother-in-law. Naomi says, "I have no home to offer
thee." Ruth replies, "Where thou lodgest, I will
lodge." Naomi says, "I go amongst an alien people."
Ruth replies, "Thy people shall be my people."

Naomi says, "I worship another God from the gods of the Moabites, the gods you have been taught to worship." Ruth replies, "Thy God shall be my God." Naomi urges, "There is no brightness in my future, no hope in my life of another husband." Ruth replies that she is content to die where Naomi dies and to share Naomi's grave. May God give to all this day the same courage, the same indomitable resolution to commit themselves to the Lord, who alone can satisfy, who alone can give eternal life.

IV

The Lord Hath Brought Me Home Again

So they two went until they came to Bethlehem. And it came to pass, when they were come to Bethlehem, that all the city was moved about them, and they said, Is this Naomi? And she said unto them, Call me not Naomi, call me Mara: for the Almighty hath dealt very bitterly with me. I went out full, and the Lord hath brought me home again empty: why then call ye me Naomi, seeing the Lord hath testified against me, and the Almighty hath afflicted me? So Naomi returned, and Ruth the Moabitess, her daughter in law, with her, which returned out of the country of Moab: and they came to Bethlehem in the beginning of barley harvest. (Ruth 1:19–22)

Weary and footsore, Naomi and Ruth finally reached the little town of Bethlehem. We read that all the city was moved about them and they said, "Is this Naomi?" About ten years had elapsed since the terrible famine when Naomi and her family emigrated to Moab. Reconstructing the scene in our imagination, we can see the women of the village lingering about the well with their waterpots, talking of the little things, as women do, when someone notices the two strangers coming down the dusty road—an elderly Hebrew woman with a younger woman of an alien race. This in itself would have attracted attention in a small town, especially in a time when travel was not the order of the day as it now is. As the strangers draw near, someone recognizes the older woman, "Is this Naomi?" Ah, what a change is here. She left us with husband and sons, hoping for a new and better life in Moab, and now she is returning alone with all the marks of poverty and care about her.

NAOMI'S DEGRADATION

As has often been observed, Naomi was undoubtedly a lady of good quality and fashion, a woman of rank and repute; otherwise her poverty would not now have been so generally noticed. Little shrubs and bushes may be grubbed to the ground and none will miss them, but who does not mark the falling of a cedar? Groveling cottages may be leveled to earth and none will take note of it, but all notice the fall of a steeple. Her former affluence now accentuated the grief and shame of her poverty. Fingers were pointed at her, eyes stared at her, words were spoken about her, the whole city was moved. They were astonished at her as she passed. No doubt many pious brows were lifted and many heads were wagged and shaken in grave rebuke. No doubt also there was pity in the ejaculation: "This, Naomi!" Naomi confesses that the impoverishing change which has come over her is from the Lord, and answers with words of pathos and bitterness, too. And she said unto them, "Call me not Naomi [that is, pleasant], call me Mara [which means bitterness]: for the Almighty hath dealt very bitterly with me."

To the ancient Hebrews, names always had significance. They were not, as is the case with us, simply designations of convenience. And at the very center of Old Testament revelation is the mysterious fact that the God of Israel has a name. You will remember that Moses said to God when he was at the burning bush, prior to his return to Egypt: "Behold, when I come unto the children of Israel, and shall say unto them, The God of your fathers hath sent me unto you; and they shall say to me, What is his name? what shall I say unto them?" (Exodus 3:13). You may recall also that the father of Samson asked of the angel who appeared unto him and to his wife, before the birth of their son, "What is thy name? . . . And the angel of the Lord said unto him, Why asketh thou thus after my name, seeing it is wonderful?" (Judges 13:17, 18). God reveals Himself throughout the Old Testament by different names, and it is a great sin and sacrilege to take the Name of the Lord in vain, because the Name of God is revelatory of God's Person and character. To despise God's Name is to despise Himself. The final and most blessed Name by which God has revealed Himself to man is the Name of Jesus.

> How sweet the Name of Jesus sounds
> In a believer's ear!
> It soothes his sorrows, heals his wounds,
> And drives away his fear.

Now Naomi reveals to us the bitterness in her heart when she says, "Call me Mara," for Mara means bitter. I am the bitter one because, "the Almighty hath dealt very bitterly with me." Here we have the weakness of human nature, the tendency to cast the blame upon God for the ill and dark providences which befall us. Way back in the beginning of the Bible we read that when God asked the first man, Adam, what he had done, though he did not deny that he was at fault, he tried to put the blame on his wife and thus really upon God. "The woman whom *thou* gavest to be with me, she gave me of the tree, and I did eat" (Genesis 3:12). It is Thy fault, O God; if Thou hadst not given me this woman, I would not have been tempted and fallen. We all have this old Adamic nature still in our hearts. We all want to call God to accounting, when the Scriptures say that His thoughts are higher than our thoughts and His ways than our ways (Isaiah 55:9), and that we should rather learn to submit ourselves in humble obedience under the mighty hand of God and be persuaded with Paul that ". . . all things work together for good to them that love God, to them who are the called according to his purpose" (Romans 8:28). Had Naomi known what would become of Ruth and how in Ruth's being blessed, her own life would again take on richness of meaning and true joy, if Naomi had only known what God intended for her, she never would have spoken thus. She had, in fact, already the token of better things in the remarkable virtue, the devotion, the genuine piety and godliness of this young Moabitess, her daughter-in-law, but her eyes were so filled with tears of bitterness and sorrow for her own calamities and losses that she could not trace the rainbow through the rain. She could not divine what a remarkable treasure she had in this young woman, her constant companion in sorrow as in joy. How much better it would have been if Naomi could have said as Job did, ". . . the Lord gave, and the Lord hath taken away; blessed be the name of the Lord" (Job 1:21).

GOD'S LOVE NEVER FAILS

It may be that you today are chafing under the hand of the Almighty, and you would reason with Him and argue the point with Him and forget that He, who loved you enough to give His Son to die for you, will not leave you at last. We should always remember and meditate upon the suffering of our Lord for us, and then we will be persuaded that a love which cost Him so much He will not lightly forget. He cannot have loved us so and leave us at last. "Yea, I have loved thee," He says, "with an everlasting love: therefore with lovingkindness have I drawn thee" (Jeremiah 31:3).

Notice that ". . . they came to Bethlehem in the beginning of barley harvest." Here the author of the book gives us a hint of better things to come. This is the first ray of light in the dawn of a new and brighter day for Ruth and Naomi, her mother-in-law. The barley harvest, according to Exodus 9:31, 32, was the first harvest of the year. In the barley sheaves we have the firstfruits of the land, and the great feast of firstfruits was celebrated in April at the conclusion of the rainy season, when the swollen river Jordan was overflowing its banks. The reason the author includes this sentence at this time is to anticipate the subsequent development of the story, for we shall see that the two women, destitute and no doubt even desperate for daily food, finally devised a bold plan according to which Ruth would go forth, though she was a stranger in the land, without the protection of father, brother, husband or son, and glean in the barley fields in order that she might find enough to keep her and her mother-in-law alive. Lesser women would have been revolted that they should be reduced to such straits, but Ruth submits with meekness and humility of character and out of her trial God makes a blessing to grow. Out of her labor comes fruit of which she could never have dreamed.

Now the New Testament speaks of the resurrected Christ as the firstfruits of them that sleep. When our Lord was crucified, dead and buried, the world of the disciples seemed to have collapsed upon their heads. They were despondent and in great despair; but out of this catastrophe, as they looked upon it, God caused joy to break in upon their hearts when He raised His Son from the dead on the third day. Have you ever had this experience of finding God gracious to you in the place and in the circumstance where you least expected Him? This has been proven over and over again to be the case on the part of men and women of faith. In their darkest hour, when they are most miserable, God has answered prayer and delivered them. Remember how Hagar, when she was cast out with her son Ishmael, because of the jealous rage of Sarah, despaired of life and left her son to die and went off to weep, that she might not behold him. Then God spoke to her; God appeared in the hour of her extremity and presented a remedy.

No doubt Naomi had to return to the home that she had left, if it was still available, though in ruins and disrepair. Or if it was occupied by another, she may have found with Ruth some little hovel on the edge of town. It must have been a desolate night, the first night back in Bethlehem, and no doubt it was a bare table to which they sat down those first days. How little did they realize what God had in store for them. But we will anticipate the story if we dwell upon that further now. I would say to any who may be in great straits and difficulties, suffering in mind or in body, and tempted to doubt the goodness of God, tempted to say with Naomi, "Call me Mara; call me bitter, for the Almighty hath dealt bitterly with me," that the cloud which you so much dread may be big with mercy and it may soon break in blessing upon your head. And to you whose sin is still upon your heart, to you whose hands are stained with wicked and evil deeds, to you whose conscience protests against you and condemns you, you who can find no peace and no rest, no happiness in life, though you may have everything that this world can give: let me speak a word to you just now. It is written: "There is no peace, saith my God, to the wicked" (Isaiah 57:21); but Jesus says, "Come unto me, all ye that labour and are heavy laden, and I will give you rest. Take my yoke upon you, and learn of me; for I am meek and lowly in heart: and ye shall find rest unto your souls" (Matthew 11:28, 29). Come back, thou prodigal son, thou wayward sinner; come back like Naomi to Bethlehem, back to the house of bread, that God may show you and reveal to you the way of deliverance, the way of sins forgiven through Christ Jesus the Lord, the only Saviour of men, who shed His blood, who gave His life that you and I might have life abundantly. And God will prove Himself to be to you a God of mercy and all comfort even as He did to Ruth and Naomi many years ago. Naomi confessed, "I went out full, and the Lord hath brought me home again empty." Confess your sin. Confess that your life is barren and empty in order that God may make it fruitful and full. Naomi had to come to the end of herself. She had to be stripped of all those things in which she trusted and hoped before God could step in and do for her what she needed most to have. Jesus said, ". . . Except a corn of wheat fall into the ground and die, it abideth alone: but if it die, it bringeth forth much fruit" (John 12:24). May God give to you this day the joy of knowing what it is to have a fruitful life in exchange for a barren one; to lose your old life that you may find a new life in Christ Jesus, the Saviour.

V

Ruth Finding Grace

And Naomi had a kinsman of her husband's, a mighty
man of wealth, of the family of Elimelech; and his name
was Boaz. And Ruth the Moabitess said unto Naomi, Let
me now go to the field, and glean ears of corn after him
in whose sight I shall find grace. And she said unto her,
Go, my daughter. And she went, and came, and gleaned
in the field after the reapers: and her hap was to light on
a part of the field belonging unto Boaz, who was of the
kindred of Elimelech.

And, behold, Boaz came from Bethlehem, and said
unto the reapers, The Lord be with you. And they answered him, The Lord bless thee. Then said Boaz unto
his servant that was set over the reapers, Whose damsel
is this? And the servant that was set over the reapers
answered and said, It is the Moabitish damsel that came
back with Naomi out of the country of Moab: And she

said, I pray you, let me glean and gather after the reapers among the sheaves: so she came, and hath continued even from the morning until now, that she tarried a little in the house. Then said Boaz unto Ruth, Hearest thou not, my daughter? Go not to glean in another field, neither go from hence, but abide here fast by my maidens: Let thine eyes be on the field that they do reap, and go thou after them: have I not charged the young men that they shall not touch thee? and when thou art athirst, go unto the vessels, and drink of that which the young men have drawn. Then she fell on her face, and bowed herself to the ground, and said unto him, Why have I found grace in thine eyes, that thou shouldest take knowledge of me, seeing I am a stranger? And Boaz answered and said unto her, It hath fully been shewed me, all that thou hast done unto thy mother in law since the death of thine husband: and how thou hast left thy father and thy mother, and the land of thy nativity, and art come unto a people which thou knewest not heretofore. The Lord recompense thy work, and a full reward be given thee of the Lord God of Israel, under whose wings thou art come to trust. (Ruth 2:1–12)

Once opulent and respected, Naomi, as we have seen, is now reduced to such sore straits that she must allow her daughter-in-law to glean amongst the reapers in quest of a morsel of bread. In fact, so severe was her want that we read later on (2:18), that Ruth set aside a portion of the food, when Boaz allowed her to have lunch with his workmen and maidens, to take home and give to her mother-in-law.

NAOMI'S KINSMAN

Now, we come to the portion of the book which tells us that "Naomi had a kinsman of her husband's, a mighty man of wealth, of the family of Elimelech; and his name was Boaz." It is not clear that Naomi referred Ruth to Boaz. In fact, it would seem that Ruth herself took the initiative, in verse 2. Having made her pledge, having taken her vow, never to leave nor forsake Naomi, she now was making good this promise. She says to Naomi, "Let me now go to the field, and glean ears of corn after him in whose sight I shall find grace." That is, "We are so destitute, I must do something. Let me go and see if I cannot find someone who will allow me, even though I am a foreigner, out of pity, to glean in his field, someone who will show me grace, that is, unmerited favor." And Naomi says unto her, "Go."

". . . weeping may endure for a night, but joy cometh in the morning" (Psalm 30:5). Now we see this Scripture fulfilled in Ruth's life by a remarkable providence of God. It says in verse 3 that she went forth and came to glean "in the field after the reapers: and her *hap* was to light on a part of the field belonging unto Boaz." "Her hap was": that is to say, it appeared from the human standpoint that this was just an accident, but we who are Christians know that there are no accidents. There is nothing that is pure chance in the life of God's people, for the God of the Scriptures is a great God who knows the end from the beginning and who orders all the affairs of our life. He makes "all things work together for good to them that love God, to them who are called according to his purpose" (Romans 8:28). It was He who guided Ruth's feet that day into this field of Boaz.

Then Boaz comes on the scene in verse 4 and we see that he is indeed a man of God, for he greets his workers with the salutation, "The Lord be with you." And they answer him, "The Lord bless thee." What a difference it would make in our relationships between employer and employee, if we had more men of God who would greet those who work for them in the Name of the Lord, and more who would labor for their employers out of a conviction that they work where God has placed them, working at their jobs with the sense of the presence of God.

We are soon aware, if we read the narrative with any care, that in Boaz Ruth has met the one who shall prove to be her salvation. He is called a mighty man of wealth. This is the same phrase used of Gideon and of Jephthah. It really means a valiant hero and it refers not simply to the power of his economic status, but rather to some brave exploits as a captain or commander of military renown, a man who is well known in his day and generation for exploits upon the field of battle. His name means "son of strength" and we shall see that he was indeed a man of great strength, not only of body but also of character; a man of high courage and conviction; a man of principle and integrity; a man who did not fear to take the right course though it was an unusual one, one which might bring criticism down upon him; a man also who was deeply religious, a fervent believer in the God of his people; a man who had the law written in his heart; a man who walked in the steps of the faith of his father Abraham and practiced this faith in the daily round and detail of life.

GOD PROTECTS RUTH

Now we begin to see God's providence unfolding, for it must have been with some reluctance that Naomi let her daughter-in-law go, and not without a sense of danger that Ruth took the risk, for reapers can be a hard lot and she might very well have met with a deadly insult. But lo, she is in the company of men who fear the Lord. Immediately Boaz notices her and asks after her and they tell him who she is. Then Boaz speaks to Ruth and tells her that she is not to glean in any other field, that she is to stay close to his own maidens. Here we have a graphic picture of an ancient harvest scene. The field is thick with waving grain, the reapers are cutting their way with sickles, filling their arms until they are full, and behind them at a respectable distance come the poor women who gather up handfuls of whatever has been dropped. Probably still farther behind is the widow and stranger, Ruth, who hesitates to associate herself too familiarly even with the poor Jewish girls, conscious of the fact that she is not one of them. There is an overseer, naturally, urging the reapers on, one from whom permission must be had even to glean. There are the great vessels of water for the thirsty laborers to refresh themselves, the barns, the threshingfloors, and the various other buildings standing at the outskirts of the field, where they may go to rest during the heat and burden of the day, lest their labor prove too great for their strength. It may be there were some shade trees here and there where men and women can gather at mealtime to eat a little parched corn mixed with vinegar, oil, and water.

And now in the midst of this scene, the master appears to see how the work goes on, and after the pious and courteous salute to his men, his eyes quickly survey this scene and he notices Ruth. It is a charming and beautiful scene of simple, pure, rural life. Already we feel that a man like Boaz is destined for a woman like Ruth. Boaz asks his overseer about her, and receives an answer. Like his master, he seems to have admired her, for he commends her for her diligence and says, verse 7, that she "hath continued even from the morning until now, that she tarried a little in the house."

Perhaps we might ask why Boaz did not volunteer to help Naomi? This we can hardly answer, for there are many circumstances now hidden to us which may have accounted for it. But we must be impressed with his integrity when we find that he had not simply listened to the gossip about town, but that he had taken pains to get to the very bottom of the matter. This in itself was a remarkable and commendable virtue. We read, in verse 11, that he told Ruth that it had been shown him all she had done for her mother-in-law since the death of her husband and how she had left her father and mother and the land of her nativity to come to a people whom she had not hither-tofore known. Rather than despising her as a for-eigner and an alien, he admires her, and we have an intuition from the start that he perceives something of the depth, the beauty, the nobility of her character. He had eyes to penetrate more deeply than Naomi her mother-in-law had done. We cannot doubt then that this man will prove her saviour. He will play the role of her kinsman-redeemer and in this respect he is a type of our Lord Jesus Christ.

JESUS, OUR BOAZ

We who are Gentiles by nature are strangers from the commonwealth of Israel and from the covenants of promise. We are, in and of ourselves, without God and without hope in the world. But Jesus, who is our Boaz, has looked upon us and loved us and has deigned to speak to us and fellowship with us, even though many of the leaders of His own people regarded the Gentiles as dogs and hated even the Samaritans who were a mixed breed—half Gentile and half Jew— and would have no dealings with them. Jesus was a friend of aliens and of strangers, and it was no more beneath Him to talk to a Samaritan woman or to grant the request of a Syro-Phoenician woman, or to commend these women for their great faith, than it was for Boaz to stoop to talk to an unknown Moabitess by the name of Ruth. And Jesus is still the friend of sinners. Jesus is still interested in those who are in need and those who are despised and rejected outcasts. It is still true that He will not break a bruised reed, He will not quench the smoking flax, and it is my prayer that as we read this story and meditate upon it and see how Ruth met Boaz, her saviour and her lord, there may be many who shall meet Jesus, the true Saviour from all sin and evil.

Boaz, having heard already of her sterling character, probably struck by her beauty as well as her humility and modest demeanor, now goes directly to Ruth and speaks with her and tells her that she should not glean in any other field, but follow his young men wherever they harvest, assuring her that they will not touch her. He urges upon her that she should feel perfectly at ease to quench her thirst from the vessels and water pots. And once again we see the character of Ruth at its best. She, who had done so much for Naomi, who had sacrificed and risked all, does not expect anyone to help her. Oh, how different this is from most of us. We do not care for others' wants, but we expect the world to help us and we become bitter and easily indulge in self-pity if we are left unnoticed. But not Ruth. She is overwhelmed by his kindness, and flings herself at his feet to pour out her thanksgiving, saying, "Why have I found grace in thine eyes, that thou shouldest take knowledge of me, seeing I am a stranger?" Is that not the way the sinner feels when he truly repents? God does not owe us anything. Can we ever cease to be amazed that He should show us His grace, we who are strangers, we who are aliens, we who are by nature afar off from Him? We deserve nothing at His hand. So long as we feel that God is owing us something, we shall never receive the supreme blessing of salvation at His hand, for it is His delight to forgive those who know that they do not deserve it. He came not to call the righteous but sinners to repentance. Have you ever heard Him calling you? Have you ever experienced in your life the grace and goodness of God and felt that you did not deserve the least of His mercies?

Boaz here shows himself to be indeed a type of our Lord for he does not now speak as a Hebrew landowner to a Moabitish vagabond and beggar, but rather he rises to the height of a Hebrew judge and prophet, one who knows that the faith of a stranger, an alien and foreigner, is acceptable to God, and he pours forth a blessing upon Ruth even as our Lord Jesus, our Boaz, has poured forth a blessing upon us. And he says, "The Lord recompense thy work, and a full reward be given thee of the Lord God of Israel, under whose wings thou art come to trust." This is the first record we have in the book that anyone in Israel had recognized Ruth, had helped her, had shown any real appreciation for her worth, for her nobility, and had offered her the privilege and blessing of the God of Israel.

So it is with our Lord. Our Lord sees the true worth and value even of the most dissolute and hopeless sinner. And, my friend, wherever you are today, though your sins may have made you an outcast from society, though your father and your mother may no longer own you to be their son, if you will seek the Lord, He will not cast you out. There has never been a man who has sunk so low but what the Lord in love will lift him. "When nothing else could help, love lifted me," the hymn-writer wrote. And that can be your experience today.

WILL YOU HEARKEN UNTO HIS WORD?

Let me call your attention to some of the steps in the narrative—steps of grace we might call them. We begin with Ruth's intention to go into the field. She does not pine away and do nothing, she seeks someone to help her. She goes out in the field and steadfastly gleans until even. As a result of this seeking, she comes face to face with one who has pity upon her; and then note how he speaks to her, "Hearest thou not, my daughter?" I want to ask you most earnestly, do you not hear the Word of the Lord? Jesus says, ". . . He that heareth my word, and believeth on him that sent me, hath everlasting life, and shall not come into condemnation; but is passed from death unto life" (John 5:24). Then Ruth hearkened unto his word, when he tells her to remain in his field, just as we should hearken unto the Word of our Lord and abide therein and not be carried to and fro by every wind of doctrine. There are different types of hearing, you know, and we have evidences of this right in the Book of Ruth. There is Orpah who hears only with the outward ear, but then she goes away to her old way of life. And so there may be some of you who hear the gospel with the outward ear, but you go on sinning and give no heed to the warnings and admonitions of the Lord. Then there are those like Naomi, who hear and who are glad enough to receive the words when all is well, but when the Lord chastens them for their waywardness, then, like the seed that is planted in shallow ground, they wither away and die. But there are those who hear with the hearing of faith as did Ruth. Boaz' words sank deeply into her heart. How is it with you? Will you be like Orpah, or Naomi, or will you let the Word of the gospel sink deeply into your heart? Will you hear the word of salvation unto the saving of your soul this day, that you may pass from death unto life and become a new creation in Christ Jesus? Oh, may God grant you grace so to hear, for His Name's sake!

VI

In the Field Until Even

*Then she said, Let me find favour in thy sight, my Lord;
for that thou hast comforted me, and for that thou hast
spoken friendly unto thine handmaid, though I be not
like unto one of thine handmaidens. And Boaz said unto
her, At mealtime come thou hither, and eat of the bread,
and dip thy morsel in the vinegar. And she sat beside the
reapers: and he reached her parched corn, and she did
eat, and was sufficed, and left. And when she was risen
up to glean, Boaz commanded his young men, saying, Let
her glean even among the sheaves, and reproach her not:
And let fall also some of the handfuls of purpose for her,
and leave them, that she may glean them, and rebuke her
not. So she gleaned in the field until even, and beat out
that she had gleaned: and it was about an ephah of barley.*

*And she took it up, and went into the city: and her
mother in law saw what she had gleaned: and she brought*

71

forth, and gave to her that she had reserved after she was sufficed. And her mother in law said unto her, Where hast thou gleaned to day? and where wroughtest thou? blessed be he that did take knowledge of thee. And she shewed her mother in law with whom she had wrought, and said, The man's name with whom I wrought to day is Boaz. And Naomi said unto her daughter in law, Blessed be he of the Lord, who hath not left off his kindness to the living and to the dead. And Naomi said unto her, The man is near of kin unto us, one of our next kinsmen. And Ruth the Moabitess said, He said unto me also, Thou shalt keep fast by my young men, until they have ended all my harvest. And Naomi said unto Ruth her daughter in law, It is good, my daughter, that thou go out with his maidens, that they meet thee not in any other field. So she kept fast by the maidens of Boaz to glean unto the end of barley harvest and of wheat harvest; and dwelt with her mother in law. (Ruth 2:13–23)

We have mentioned the steps of grace which Ruth took until she found her deliverer, her Boaz, the one who showed her favor and kindness, the one in whose eyes she found grace. Let us continue our analysis of this fascinating story and draw those lessons from it which God the Holy Spirit would have us learn.

Our text begins with Ruth's acknowledgment of joy that Boaz should speak words of comfort to her and show himself friendly toward her though she is not one of his handmaidens. She utters no reproach against the inhabitants of Bethlehem for having left her unprovided, for having left her to her own resources, but she is full of gratitude that Boaz should show her a friendly recognition in the midst of her isolation, in the midst of unsympathetic and suspicious neighbors. This apparently warmed his heart toward her the more. Here he perceived indeed a virtue rarely found, a tenderness and responsiveness that was of great price, a fidelity which could not but provoke his sensitive response and admiration. He seems to feel like our Lord felt about those outside of Israel who had great faith, when He was constrained to say upon occasion, "I have not found so great faith, no, not in Israel" (Matthew 8:10). Here Boaz sees a beauty which has not been appreciated, which has not enlisted the sympathy nor won the response of those amongst whom Ruth has lived and moved. But *he* responds, and he answers her kindly and tells her that at mealtime she is to come and eat bread and dip her morsel in the vinegar and sit beside the reapers. This she did and ate until she was sufficed. Here we have some of the Oriental customs, many of which are referred to throughout the book. We will look at some of these customs later on. Suffice it to say, that it was very unusual for a landlord to extend such an invitation as this. And that is the experience we have had by the grace of God, is it not—we who are born aliens and strangers from the commonwealth of Israel? We have been made to sit down with Abraham, Isaac and Jacob in the kingdom. We have been invited to feast at the table of the Lord with His own chosen people, until our souls shall be sufficed.

THE LORD'S GRACE

Boaz is not satisfied simply with this gesture of kindness. He commands his young men that they shall let her glean, even among the sheaves, and reproach her not. In fact they shall let some handfuls fall on purpose for her that she may glean them. They are to say nothing to her that would put her to the blush, nothing that would shame and abash her. They are to reprove her in no way. And so it is with us.

When we come unto the Lord and find grace and favor in His sight, He does for us more than we can ask or think. Is it not so? He not only invites us to feast at His table, but He gives us special blessings in His providence—handfuls on purpose of good things, and tender mercies, all of them foretastes of even better things to come.

"O YE OF LITTLE FAITH"

Now amid all these favors Ruth does not lose her head. She does not become overly confident. She does not become self-centered. She thinks of her hungry mother-in-law and, though she has satisfied her own needs, she does not forget to lay aside a portion of food for Naomi. Nor does she stint in her labor because of the kindness of Boaz who made it easier for her. She continues to work with diligence and purpose and steadfastness of mind until evening and beats out her gleanings until she has nearly a bushel (an ephah) of barley to carry home. When she arrives home, her mother-in-law is amazed at what she sees and says, "Where hast thou gleaned today?" And we cannot but expect Naomi to be most surprised and happy at such an unexpected turn of fortune. It is probably not too much to suppose that she had been apprehensive all day, home alone with nothing but her needs, her poverty, her want, four bare walls staring her in the face, uncertain what would happen to Ruth. She was undoubtedly tempted to imagine the worst, and hardly could find it in her heart to hope for the good, but now God rebukes her little faith, just as our Lord rebuked the little faith of His disciples who were fearful in the time of need and called upon Him when they were in the storm, crying out that they were about to perish (Luke 8:24, 25). Even though they had seen His good hand upon them, they still did not have the faith to trust Him. How is it with you today? Will you trust the Lord in the dark hour even as in the noonday?

"BUT JOY COMETH IN THE MORNING"

Naomi hardly gives Ruth time to answer. She goes on to bless the man, whoever he may be, who has shown her such kindness. The man who had treated her beloved daughter so well, had weighted her down with all this barley and thus rewarded her toils, had done a good deed and she readily invokes a blessing upon his head. Then Ruth tells her story of the day and it is summed up in verse 19. She tells her mother-in-law with whom she had labored and she tells her his name, "The man's name with whom I wrought to day is Boaz." It would appear that she did not know what the sound of his name would mean to Naomi, but Naomi grasps the situation at once and cries out, "Blessed be he of the Lord, who hath not left off his kindness to the living and to the dead. And Naomi said unto her, The man is near of kin unto us, one of our next kinsmen." Evidently Naomi saw in this a token of the fact that God had not abandoned her after all, that He had not left off His kindness toward her as she had supposed. Now her soul is moved from despair to renewed hope in the divine goodness and compassion. And we cannot but feel that Boaz must have been happy that night in doing the good that he had done. There is no greater joy in life than playing the role of the good Samaritan, in showing compassionate kindness to our neighbors in trouble and in any want. This is our responsibility, our duty and our privilege for we are to "love our neighbor as ourself." Have you shown kindness to those in need? Have you shared the happiness which is yours and the joy which is yours in Christ with those who are destitute? Have you given of your means to help to feed the poor? The Lord tells us that if we so much as give a cup of cold water in His Name, we shall not fail of our reward. The Lord will remember our kindness. Boaz was rich and the few extra handfuls of barley which he commanded his servants, the harvesters, to give to Ruth was nothing. And yet what rich dividends it must have paid in his conscience and in his soul. You can give a little and receive much if you have the will to bless those and help those who are in need. Boaz spoke kindly to Ruth. May God give us all lips to speak a word in season, a word of comfort, encouragement and help, especially to point sinners to Christ who is the only Saviour from sin, before it is too late.

FAITHFUL STEWARDSHIP

Up to now we have considered the various steps of grace which Ruth followed, how she went out in her need in quest of help, how in the providence of God she was brought to glean in the field of Boaz, and how she demeaned herself with such modesty and humility that Boaz was moved with pity and compassion and spoke to her kindly and told his young men to help her. Now I want you to notice some additional phases of Ruth's growth in grace, as it were, and how she is a type of the Christian pilgrim on his wilderness journey to the promised land. Notice first of all her steadfastness, how she gleaned in the field until eventide, keeping fast by the maidens of Boaz, and how she went and dwelt with her mother-in-law and remained faithful to her and provided for her. This steadfastness of Ruth, a wonderful mark of her character, is a type of the steadfastness which should mark every true believer in Christ. The Scriptures exhort us to be "stedfast, unmoveable, always abounding in the work of the Lord . . ." (I Corinthians 15:58), so that we will not be carried away by every whim of doctrine. Let us be rooted and grounded and built up in the Word according to the admonition of Scripture. You will notice also that Ruth faithfully gleaned until she had approximately a bushel of barley. Here again there is a spiritual truth for those whose eyes are opened by the Holy Spirit. As Ruth gleaned in the fields of Boaz, so we should glean in the field of God's Word. Oh, do not be in a hurry to leave off reading the Word of God! Like Ruth who gleaned until even, gleaned until she had a large quantity of food, so spend time with God's Word. As the hymn-writer advises: "Take time to be holy, Speak oft with thy Lord; Abide in Him always, And feed on His Word." As a result of her gleaning, she had much grain to beat out and thresh until it was pure and clean from all chaff. So we also should glean and beat out the truth of God's Word. We are admonished to search the Scripture just as Joseph's steward searched for his master's cup in Benjamin's sack, searched until he had found it. Just as Joshua gives instructions to the spies that they are to search out the land and find out all about it, so we should search the Scriptures daily. We read in Acts 17:11 that the Bereans "were more noble than those in Thessalonica, in that they received the word with all readiness of mind, and searched the scriptures daily, whether those things were so." We live in a day and in a land where there are many false teachings and cults abroad because men have not studied the Word. They are not trained in the doctrines of truth and they have no way of discerning what is right. And I say unto you that if you would know the truth, then "Study to shew thyself approved unto God, a workman that needeth not to be ashamed, rightly dividing the word of truth" (II Timothy 2:15).

STRENGTH IN GOD'S WORD

You will notice further that Ruth had, as a result of her gleaning, an abundance of grain. She had more than she needed for that day; you also need a reserve in your hearts of the Word of God for the evil day, whenever it may come. As we are exhorted in Colossians 3:16, we should let the Word of Christ dwell in us richly in all wisdom. In my years of experience as a minister of the gospel, many times I have seen some fiery trial, some severe testing, come upon the saints of God, and it has been wonderful to behold them in this situation, in the hour of trial and loneliness with aching heart, drawing upon the reserves of God's precious Word which is the food of their souls. They have treasured it up in days past as an incorruptible seed and now, when testing comes and they enter into tribulation, they find this Word gives them strength for all their troubles and trials.

You will pardon, will you not, a personal reference. I shall never forget how nearly forty years ago on a Saturday night my mother was very low, and early Sunday morning she slipped away to be with the

Lord. My father and I were seated in the living room and Dad said to me, "Get down the Bible, Charles, and let us find what God has to say about what happens after death. Let us just find out once again." So we turned to John 11:25, 26: "I am the resurrection, and the life: he that believeth in me, though he were dead, yet shall he live: And whosoever liveth and believeth in me shall never die." Then we turned also to John 14:1, 2 and read those words, "Let not your heart be troubled: ye believe in God, believe also in me. In my Father's house are many mansions. . . ." And in II Corinthians 5:1 we read, "For we know that if our earthly house of this tabernacle were dissolved, we have a building of God, an house not made with hands, eternal in the heavens." I shall never forget that night as we went over the Word of God and as we drew upon the reserves of God's Word to meet our need in the hour of trial. How I thanked the Lord that as we laid away my mother in the grave, I had the comfort and the promise of His Word, that I need not sorrow as those that have no hope. God has given unto His people in the Scriptures exceeding great and precious promises. Do you, my friend, know these promises? Have you ever appropriated them?

Have you ever learned to store the Word of God in your heart that you might have a reserve in the hour and in the day of need; that you might be made a partaker of the divine nature and escape the corruption which is in the world through lust?

You will observe finally that Naomi takes notice of Ruth's abundance of grain. She is immediately impressed the moment Ruth steps in the door that she should have so much, and asks her about it. And if you are a real student of the Word of God, if you feed your soul upon the bread of life, if you faithfully study the Scriptures, people will see the difference in your life, people will see that you have been with the Lord. If the Word of God dwells in your life richly, your neighbors and friends will notice it. They will see that you have been with Jesus. As we close this meditation, I would simply ask you this question with all seriousness and earnestness, What about your life? Do you have reserves of spiritual power? Can men and women, when they live with you, see that you have been with the Lord? Do you know the Lord as your Saviour? Have you met your Boaz and gleaned in the field of His Word; or is your life empty? Have you nothing to show for your labor but the husks of this world's vain pleasures; the gold and silver which is corrupted by rust? Will you not cast aside all these things and take the great treasure, the treasure of great price, the salvation which is offered you in the gospel freely and this day cast yourself upon the mercy of God in Christ? Then you, like Ruth, though you be poor, yet you will become rich; though you were hungry, yet you will now have all that your soul can desire and the hope of heaven too.

VII

In the Threshingfloor

Then Naomi her mother in law said unto her, My daughter, shall I not seek rest for thee, that it may be well with thee? And now is not Boaz of our kindred, with whose maidens thou wast? Behold, he winnoweth barley to night in the threshingfloor. Wash thyself therefore, and anoint thee, and put thy raiment upon thee, and get thee down to the floor: but make not thyself known unto the man, until he shall have done eating and drinking. And it shall be, when he lieth down, that thou shalt mark the place where he shall lie, and thou shalt go in, and uncover his feet, and lay thee down; and he will tell thee what thou shalt do. And she said unto her, All that thou sayest unto me I will do.

And she went down unto the floor, and did according to all that her mother in law bade her. And when Boaz had eaten and drunk, and his heart was merry, he went *to lie down at the end of the heap of corn: and she came softly, and uncovered his feet, and laid her down. (Ruth 3:1–7)*

Chapter 3 of the Book of Ruth brings us to a dramatic climax. The scene is shifted from the barley field to the threshingfloor and the curtain of the centuries is pulled back as we are given one of the most intimate glimpses of ancient custom and usage to be found anywhere in the whole Bible. Perhaps the incident recorded in this chapter has seemed to you somewhat difficult, as though there might be here a touch of impropriety if not impurity in that which is done. But if we feel that Ruth and her mother-in-law are guilty of any immodesty or boldness, or that Boaz is lacking in any honor or virtue, it is because we are so far removed in our present standards and conventions from our hero and his bride-to-be. We do them an injustice if we forget that they are thirty centuries removed from us. And if we have the eyes to see it, we will discern that there is here a patriarchal simplicity of manners and custom which in its nobility

and purity really transcends our own age in many
respects.

RUTH'S LEGAL CLAIM

To understand the counsel of Naomi to Ruth, her
daughter-in-law, we need to remember that the law
of Moses, according to Deuteronomy 25:5, specified
that if the brethren dwell together and one of them
die having no children, the wife of the dead shall not
marry a stranger, but her husband's brother shall go
in unto her and take her to him to wife and perform
the duties of a husband's brother to her in order that
he may raise up seed to the name of his brother. This
explains what we read here in Ruth 3. Ruth, creeping
softly into the resting place of Boaz on the threshingfloor and lying down next to Boaz, is simply making
a legal claim in the manner of her time. No doubt the
plan was a somewhat hazardous one, for we are told
expressly that the heart of Boaz was cheerful with
wine when Ruth came in to him. She would have to
trust that the virtue of the man was such that he
would be able to master both inclination and opportunity and to withstand all temptation and never
betray the confidence which she had reposed in him.

We can see from the way he answered her, when he discovered who she was and her true design, that he was worthy of her trust, for there was a simple piety and a tenderness in his tone as he called her "daughter," and a purity of heart as he invoked upon her the blessing of God.

A HAVEN OF REST

Now as we turn to the text, I want you to notice the word "rest" in the first verse. Naomi says, "Shall I not seek rest for thee?" This simply means a place of peace, freedom and honor, which, for the Hebrew woman, could be found only in the house of her husband. Hence, the Hebrews would speak of this home as the woman's rest, the secure and happy asylum from neglect or servitude. In like manner, the whole nation was taught to look upon the land of Canaan in which they sojourned as God's rest. Moses says, while the Israelites are still wandering in the wilderness, "For ye are not as yet come to the rest and to the inheritance, which the Lord your God giveth you" (Deuteronomy 12:9). Here we have a beautiful type of the rest which is laid up for the believer in Jesus. As Naomi sought rest for Ruth, her daughter-in-law, in the house of Boaz, so should the sinner seek rest from all his sin at the hand of Jesus, the Boaz of His people, for He says, "Come unto me, all ye that labour and are heavy laden, and I will give you rest" (Matthew 11:28). Naomi's action reveals to us that she at last perceived that her daughter-in-law was indeed come to be a true Israelite. Boaz himself had blessed her for having taken shelter under the wings of the Lord God of Israel and having come to trust in His Name. Naomi now understands that the darkness of Ruth's lot, which she had feared when Ruth returned with her to Bethlehem, has been turned into light by the mercy and providence of God. Therefore, Naomi takes courage to seek a home for Ruth who had loved her with a rare and virtuous love. It is also significant that Ruth had the wisdom to follow Naomi's advice in the light of Boaz' age. It would appear from what he says to Ruth in verse 10, that he was an older man and that he was greatly surprised that she had not sought out a husband among the younger men, whether poor or rich.

OUR KINSMAN-REDEEMER

Another word that we need to notice is the word for kinsman in verse 9. When Ruth speaks to Boaz in the darkness of the threshingfloor, she says, ". . . thou art a near kinsman." This word really means one who unlooses that which has been bound, restores it to its original position. It can be used to describe one, for example, who redeems a piece of land by paying any mortgage against it and then gives it back to its original owner; or one who gives a ransom to release a captive in order that he may set him free. The basic idea is that of loosing one who has been bound. This is the meaning of the word as applied here. According to the Jewish law, as we have seen, if a man died without issue, his nearest kin was to marry his widow in order that the family might not become extinct, for the families of the land by holding the land inherited from their ancestors, through the generations trained their children in the pious customs and religious beliefs of the fathers as God had revealed them, and this was essential to the well-being of the nation. By this act, then, of marrying one's widowed sister-in-law, families were preserved from extinction and sons were provided who should have the name and possession of the first husband. Thus the kinsman redeems his brother's name and his inheritance from being blotted out and being lost. As we have said before, in this regard Boaz is a type of Christ, our Kinsman-Redeemer. No Israelite who might lose his fields because he did not have a son to inherit from him ever could have a loss comparable with ours; for by our sins we have lost our claims to heaven, we have lost our right to become the sons of God, we have fallen short of the glory of God—and who shall deliver us and lift up our heads and restore to us our inheritance in the Lord? Who will bring us back into the fold? Who, but the Lord Jesus Christ, our Kinsman-Redeemer. Have you sought Him out as Ruth did Boaz? He will become your Kinsman, making you an heir of God and a joint-heir with Himself.

OUR OWN RIGHTEOUSNESS AS FILTHY RAGS

Now notice what Naomi tells Ruth to do, "Wash thyself." Like Ruth, we need to be washed, for we are sinners. Now only the blood of Jesus Christ, God's Son, can cleanse us from all sin (I John 1:7). Then she is to anoint herself. In the Book of the Revelation the church of Laodicea received a letter from the Lord, in which He accused them of boasting that they are rich and have need of nothing. But the Lord says to them that they really are poor, blind and naked, though they know it not, and counselled them to buy of Him gold tried in the fire that they may be truly rich and to anoint their eyes with eye-salve that they might truly see. Do you know what it is to have the anointing of the Holy Spirit, so that your eyes are opened to see yourself as you truly are, a sinner; to recognize all your righteous works as filthy rags in the eyes of God; to look upon Jesus as the Son of God and your Saviour and to cast yourself upon His mercy and plead for salvation through His blood? As you read the Word of God, always be sure to pray the Holy Spirit that He will anoint the eyes of your under-standing that you, being enlightened, may see things eternal, things spiritual and that the things of this world which are temporal and passing may seem of little account and of little value to you.

Please notice finally, how Naomi tells Ruth to put on her raiment. In this respect also she is a type of the believer, the one who finds in Christ his Kinsman-Redeemer and puts on the robes of His righteousness. We can never go to heaven wearing our own raiment. It is not good enough. The prophet Isaiah compares it to filthy rags. You remember the parable of the great wedding feast and how one man came in not having on a wedding garment and the lord of the feast said unto him, "Friend, how camest thou in hither not having a wedding garment? And he was speechless. Then said the king to the servants, Bind him hand and foot, and take him away, and cast him into outer darkness; there shall be weeping and gnashing of teeth" (Matthew 22:12, 13). In Ephesians 4:22–24 we read, ". . . put off concerning the former conversation the old man, which is corrupt according to the deceitful lusts; And be renewed in the spirit of your mind; And that ye put on the new man, which after God is created in righteousness and true holiness." This, says Paul, is the truth as it is in Jesus. Oh, how we need to live in the reality of this truth, that if we have any part in Christ, we should be daily prepared to meet Him as our heavenly Bridegroom, that we should put off from us all those things which are displeasing to Him, and that we should put on the new man which is renewed in knowledge after the image of Him that created him. The filthy rags of our self-righteousness must be replaced with the clothing of meekness and righteousness in Christ. Sinner, I plead with you earnestly, do not procrastinate, do not delay, do not put off these things, for in an hour that ye think not the Son of Man cometh and the door will be closed. Then it will be too late to enter into the inheritance of the saints.

OBEDIENCE A NECESSITY

Finally, notice how obedient Ruth was. She said in verse 5 to her mother-in-law, "All that thou sayest unto me I will do." And she went down unto the threshingfloor and uncovered the feet of Boaz and laid herself down at his feet as a sign of her subjection to him and of her willingness to become his handmaid, his servant, his espoused wife. May God give each one of us obedient hearts to do as Ruth did, that we may put away our evil works, and having the anointing of the Holy Spirit may put on the robes of Christ's righteousness and be prepared to meet Him when, as our heavenly Bridegroom, He shall come and take us unto Himself.

VIII

Ruth Resting

And now, my daughter, fear not; I will do to thee all that
thou requirest: for all the city of my people doth know
that thou art a virtuous woman. And now it is true that
I am thy near kinsman: howbeit there is a kinsman nearer
than I. Tarry this night, and it shall be in the morning,
that if he will perform unto thee the part of a kinsman,
well; let him do the kinsman's part: but if he will not do
the part of a kinsman to thee, then will I do the part of a
kinsman to thee, as the Lord liveth: lie down until the
morning.

And she lay at his feet until the morning: and she rose
up before one could know another. And he said, Let it not
be known that a woman came into the floor. Also he said,
Bring the veil that thou hast upon thee, and hold it. And
when she held it, he measured six measures of barley,
and laid it on her: and she went into the city. And when

she came to her mother in law, she said, Who art thou, my daughter? And she told her all that the man had done to her. And she said, These six measures of barley gave he me; for he said to me, Go not empty unto thy mother in law. Then she said, Sit still, my daughter, until thou know how the matter will fall: for the man will not be in rest, until he have finished the thing this day. (Ruth 3:11–18)

In our former meditation we saw how Ruth, in obedience to Naomi's instructions, went down to the threshingfloor at night. This was at the time when Boaz had laid himself down, foreshadowing Christ, our Kinsman-Redeemer, who laid His life down in death for us, a divine sin offering and substitute, bearing our sins in His body on the tree. We saw how she drew near unto him to uncover his feet. So may we draw near unto Christ and uncover His feet to see the marks of the cruel nails that pierced those feet, to gaze upon the wounds of Calvary, and to remember that "He was wounded for our transgressions, he was bruised for our iniquities: the chastisement of our peace was upon him; and with his stripes we are healed" (Isaiah 53:5).

RUTH IS ENCOURAGED

Now let us consider the outcome of Ruth's obedience, and the response of Boaz when she told him who she was, reminded him that she was near of kin, and asked him to spread his skirt over her as his handmaid. This is indeed a dramatic moment in our story and one that must have been fraught with deep emotion for Ruth. She may have asked herself the question, "What will Boaz say? Will he accept me, will he receive me?" And there may be someone who reads this Book of Ruth who is in doubt in his heart, who cannot believe that the Lord will become to him his Kinsman-Redeemer. Let me remind you, my friend, that Jesus said, "All that the Father giveth me shall come to me: and him that cometh to me I will in no wise cast out" (John 6:37). Boaz did not reckon that he had done all that he could for Ruth because he had allowed her to glean in his fields and had given her a share with his reapers. Rather he answered Ruth with great comfort and encouragement and pronounced the blessing of the Lord upon her for what she had done: "Now, my daughter, fear not; I will do to thee all that thou requirest." So the Lord speaks to everyone who seeks

His face: "Sinner, fear not, I will do to thee all that thou requirest; yea, even more than thou canst ask or even think."

A NEARER KINSMAN

At this point in our story an interesting development occurs. We discover that though Boaz is indeed a near kinsman, there is one who is nearer than he. The ancient custom and law that no Hebrew family should be allowed to lapse, but rather that each house should be maintained in its land and possession, that the nearest of kin should protect the widow and raise up seed by her that the name of her husband should not die in Israel—this ancient law and custom Boaz declares he will be happy to fulfill. But he must stand aside and give another the first opportunity. This, no doubt, is one of the reasons why Boaz had not taken the initiative. We need not suppose that Naomi was unaware of the facts or that Ruth was either. Rather it would seem most likely that Naomi ventured to approach Boaz since he would feel some impediment in taking the first step himself. Thus she gave this counsel out of love to her daughter-in-law, in order to help Ruth to obtain a husband who would not only be able to help her in material matters, but also, as a devout man, would provide for her and her children a godly home.

It is very important that parents, guardians and elders should take into account the spiritual well-being of their children and those who are in their charge, when it comes to advising and counselling, and helping them in marriage. This is one of the most important decisions in life and oftentimes young people are in want of that mature wisdom which age brings. How fortunate was Ruth that she had such counsel and how wise she shows herself to be, in that she chose to obey it.

BOAZ' PROMISE

Now turning to Boaz' promise, you will notice that he binds himself with an oath saying, in effect: "As the Lord liveth, I will do the part of a kinsman to thee. If he who is nearest of kin refuse thee the duty and honor, then I, Boaz, shall redeem thy dead husband's name and inheritance." Probably Boaz found it difficult to tell her of this nearer kinsman. We may presume, since he referred to younger men, that he was deeply attached to Ruth, but that there was another kinsman younger than himself who had the first claim to her. Again Boaz proved the nobility of his character and the integrity and honor of his person by his resolve to give the nearer kinsman his legal due, although it would be to him a great sacrifice to lose Ruth. There is a kind of quiet heroism in the man at this point.

You will notice, furthermore, that Boaz resolved to set about the affair at once. He instructed Ruth to tarry there on the threshingfloor that night, promising that in the morning he would see whether or not her nearest kinsman would redeem her. If not, then he would surely do so immediately. So it is with the Lord Jesus. When the sinner comes to Christ, there is no delay; the Lord's ear is ever inclined unto the sinner's cry for help, and He anticipates, as it were, our need and provides a remedy as soon as we make suit for it.

Boaz made sure that Ruth left before the day sprang up into light, lest anyone might have seen her and a breath of suspicion might have blown over her, causing her to be victimized by some cruel gossip. Yet before she went he made her take off her shawl and hold it while he poured barley into it. Then she turned and went homeward, bearing her heavy burden with a light heart. Even this has more to it than meets the eye, for no doubt Boaz gave Ruth this grain not simply to provide for her needs, but that she would appear, in the event that anyone met her in the way, to have been gleaning early in the fields, and thus allay all suspicion and question from the mind of any over-curious neighbor about their private interview.

Notice also that Boaz gave Ruth *six measures* of barley. Why is this number six mentioned? Six does have a symbolical meaning and it appears that Naomi was quick to read it, for when Ruth returned, she told her mother-in-law, "These six measures of barley gave he me." Whereupon Naomi replied: "Sit still, my daughter, until thou know how the matter will fall: for the man will not be in rest, until he have finished the thing this day." The number six, we are told, is a symbol of labor and service among the Hebrews, and it is followed by seven as a symbol of rest and per-fection. God labored six days to make heaven and earth and rested on the seventh. So the Israelites tilled the earth diligently for six days as an agricultural people and rested on the seventh day; and every seventh year they were to give the land itself a sab-batical rest. So Naomi apparently felt that there was here a hint that Boaz would not rest until his labor was finished. He would be busy about the matter until he had settled it once and for all. Therefore, she bade Ruth to stay at home until he came to fetch her to be his bride, to wait patiently for him until all legal matters had been settled; for she was confident that he would not allow any grass to grow under his feet until he had redeemed Ruth, until he had found rest for her in his home.

THE CHRISTIAN'S HOPE

And so we as Christians waiting for our heavenly Boaz should rest here until He comes, and wait patiently for Him, being assured that the promise which He has made to be about our salvation, to prepare for us mansions in glory—this promise He surely will fulfill. When the time has come He will rend the heavens, and with the voice of the archangel and the trump of God, He will descend to take us unto Himself. Sometimes we as Christians find it very difficult to wait for the Lord. We grow weary with our waiting; we fall asleep like the virgins, we do not watch in faith. But let us ". . . lift up the hands which hang down, and the feeble knees" (Hebrews 12:12). Let us rest in this confidence that what the Lord has promised, He is able also to perform, and that one day soon Jesus will come and receive us unto Himself. In all the trials of life let this hope be an anchor to our souls, that soon our labors and troubles shall be over and He shall take us to be with Himself, safe on that beautiful shore.

IX

Then Went Boaz Up to the Gate

*Then went Boaz up to the gate, and sat him down there:
and, behold, the kinsman of whom Boaz spake came by;
unto whom he said, Ho, such a one! turn aside, sit down
here. And he turned aside, and sat down. And he took ten
men of the elders of the city, and said, Sit ye down here.
And they sat down. And he said unto the kinsman, Naomi,
that is come again out of the country of Moab, selleth a
parcel of land, which was our brother Elimelech's: And
I thought to advertise thee, saying, Buy it before the inhabitants, and before the elders of my people. If thou wilt
redeem it, redeem it: but if thou wilt not redeem it, then
tell me, that I may know: for there is none to redeem it
beside thee; and I am after thee. And he said, I will redeem it. Then said Boaz, What day thou buyest the field
of the hand of Naomi, thou must buy it also of Ruth the*

Moabitess, the wife of the dead, to raise up the name of the dead upon his inheritance.

And the kinsman said, I cannot redeem it for myself, lest I mar mine own inheritance: redeem thou my right to thyself; for I cannot redeem it. (Ruth 4:1–6)

In ancient times before the days of guided missiles and long-range bombers, the best way of protecting a city was to build a wall about it. As a result there were hundreds of walled cities and towns scattered all over Israel with huge gates which could be closed up at night or fastened tightly shut in the event an enemy appeared on the horizon. A comparatively small entrance could be defended much more effectively than the entire borders of a city, as would have been required had there been no walls. The gates of ancient cities played many other roles. They served as market places, as courts of justice, and business was often deliberated and transacted there. Some of them were massive structures with little ante-chambers furnished for reclining and for conversation. Here the inhabitants of the city would assemble to transact their business, to hear and tell the news. Here also judges would sit to administer justice to all comers. This is the scene in the fourth and last chapter of the Book of Ruth. The transactions we are about to discuss took place at one of the gates of the city of Bethlehem. The Book of Ruth opened in the harvest field; then the scene shifted to the threshingfloor. Now once more it changes and we are at the gate of the city.

THE ANCIENT CUSTOM

In this Book of Ruth we have, as it were, a cabinet full of ancient customs and usages. Let us follow Boaz to the gate and mark with care how he proceeds in his legal suit, noticing the simplicity of the ancient Hebrew customs and yet their dignified formality. We must remember the law of the kinsman-redeemer which we have mentioned before; how the nearest of kin must marry a childless widow, that the son born of her in due time may enter into the inheritance and perpetuate the name of his mother's first husband. (See Deuteronomy 25:5–10.) Now as we sit down with Boaz at the gate, it is very early in the morning, for he hurried there from the threshingfloor, as he had promised Ruth he would, in order to get the business at hand settled as soon as possible. He has not been sitting there very long before the nearer kinsman passes by. Boaz hails him, using, apparently, a legal form of summons to make it plain that he has some business to transact: "Ho, such a one! turn aside, sit down here." And so the man obeys. As he watches the citizens passing in and out of the gate, Boaz asks now one and now another of the elders to sit down with them until he has gathered together ten (a legal number) of the best-reputed men of Bethlehem to be witnesses and judges of the case. Undoubtedly many people, seeing the wealthy and pious Boaz with so many grave elders assembled, realize that some important business is about to be transacted and they, too, stop to see what is going to happen.

WILT THOU REDEEM IT?

Boaz opens the proceedings very formally by announcing that Naomi is about to sell a piece of land belonging to Elimelech. This means that the kinsman is legally bound to buy this land, and that, since Naomi is past the age for having children, he must marry Ruth who shares a claim in Naomi's family. We find that there is no argument about this. The kinsman

of Naomi admits the claim and, so long as he thinks
he may have only to redeem the land that is in question, he is willing to satisfy the requirement and to
pay the money necessary to keep the land in the
possession of Elimelech's family. When the question
is put to him, "Wilt thou redeem it?" he answers, "I
will."

Knowing, as we do, that Boaz loves Ruth and hopes
to have her to wife, we may suppose that he receives
this reply with some dismay. But he has one resource
left: the kinsman is bound to marry Ruth, but he may
not wish to do so. Boaz therefore quickly rejoins, in
effect, "If you redeem the land of Elimelech and keep
it for Naomi, you must also take Ruth, the Moabitess,
and raise up seed to Naomi's son, who has died, that
he may not lose his inheritance. Are you also prepared
to do this?" At this point the nearest of kin demurs
and refuses to go through with the transaction. The
law says that under such circumstances the widow
who is spurned may spit in the man's face, but evidently Boaz wished to make it easier for him to de-
cline Ruth by not bringing her with him. Also, Boaz
has made it perfectly plain that he is willing to dis-
charge all the duties of the near of kin, if this other

man declines them. Therefore, we may suppose that he not only spares his near kinsman embarrassment by not carrying out the letter of the law, but also he is moved out of love for Ruth and his desire to have her for himself.

It may also be, since Ruth was a proselyte, a Jewess by choice only and not by birth, that the law was doubtful and Boaz does not feel that he should push things too far in forcing the hand of his near of kin. This may also be a reason why Ruth and Naomi are not present at this transaction and are not called upon to contemn the man by spitting in his face. Perhaps, too, that is what the kinsman means when he says, "I cannot redeem it for myself, lest I mar mine own inheritance." He may be suggesting that there is some question in his mind as to the propriety of marrying a foreign woman. Boaz, however, has no such feeling, for he knows Ruth well and knows that she has the heart of a devout and godly Jewess, even though she has the blood of a Moabitess in her veins. Perhaps Boaz knew from the start that his kinsman had such qualms and now decides to make the most of it, hoping the man will refuse Ruth. He challenges him, therefore, stressing her alien birth as he reminds the man that he must not only buy the land, but also take Ruth the *Moabitess* to be his wife to raise up a son to the name of the dead and to his inheritance. So the anonymous kinsman refuses to redeem Ruth with her inheritance and cedes all rights to Boaz.

THE CHRISTIAN'S INHERITANCE

Now notice how energetically Boaz conducted this whole matter, how open and straightforward he was in the transaction. In this he was a type of our Lord and foreshadowed the work of our Lord. As Boaz went up to the gate and sat down, so our Lord Jesus Christ ascended up into heaven and is seated at the right hand of the Father in the place of all authority and power in order that He might enter into heaven itself as our Redeemer, there to plead our case and secure our inheritance.

Remember also that according to II Samuel 23:8–17, there was a famous well of water at this gate of Bethlehem where Boaz went. It was a well of water from which David had frequently drawn, and when he was with his mighty men fleeing Saul and hiding in the wilderness, he longed for a drink at that well. Three of his chief men who were with him in the cave of Adullam risked their lives to bring him this water. To David's honor it must be recorded that, since he realized his men had put their lives in jeopardy to bring him this water, he would not drink it, but poured it out as an offering to the Lord. As Boaz went to the gate where the water of Bethlehem was, so our ascended Lord gives the water of life freely to all those who will come to drink. As He was speaking to His disciples during the last great day of the feast in Jerusalem, He said: "If any man thirst, let him come unto me, and drink. He that believeth on me, as the scripture hath said, out of his belly shall flow rivers of living water. (But this spake he of the Spirit, which they that believe on him should receive: for the Holy Ghost was not yet given)" (John 7:37–39). You cannot obtain the water of life except you come to Him who sits at His Father's right hand and who has poured out the promise of the Spirit upon all those who trust in Him. Have you ever tasted of this water? Do you have the Spirit of life, the Spirit of Christ? Paul says, "If any man have not the Spirit of Christ, he is none of his. . . . For as many as are led by the Spirit of God, they are the sons of God " (Romans 8:9, 14).

THE REDEMPTION WHICH IS IN CHRIST

In closing I would have you notice the impotence of the nearest of kin to carry out his obligation. He said, "I cannot redeem it for myself." In this he is a type of the law. The law is rendered impotent by our sins. The law is unable to redeem us and save us. By the works of the law there shall no flesh be justified, and therefore we can never hope to be *saved* by seeking to keep the law. We must be delivered from the law as a way of salvation, by our Saviour, Jesus Christ. He has been made a curse for us: ". . . for it is written, Cursed is every one that hangeth on a tree: That the blessing of Abraham might come on the Gentiles through Jesus Christ; that we might receive the promise of the Spirit through faith" (Galatians 3:13, 14). Christ then, like Boaz, comes in to do for us what the nearest of kin cannot do. May God give you grace to cease striving after the righteousness which is in the law, in order that you may find that righteousness and redemption which is in Christ and find Him as your personal Saviour, who alone can save from sin both now and forever.

X

He Plucked Off His Shoe

Now this was the manner in former time in Israel concerning redeeming and concerning changing, for to confirm all things; a man plucked off his shoe, and gave it to his neighbour: and this was a testimony in Israel. Therefore the kinsman said unto Boaz, Buy it for thee. So he drew off his shoe.

And Boaz said unto the elders, and unto all the people, Ye are witnesses this day, that I have bought all that was Elimelech's, and all that was Chilion's and Mahlon's, of the hand of Naomi. Moreover Ruth the Moabitess, the wife of Mahlon, have I purchased to be my wife, to raise up the name of the dead upon his inheritance, that the name of the dead be not cut off from among his brethren, and from the gate of his place: ye are witnesses this day. And all the people that were in the gate, and the elders, *said, We are witnesses. The Lord make the woman that is come into thine house like Rachel and like Leah, which two did build the house of Israel: and do thou worthily in Ephratah, and be famous in Bethlehem: And let thy house be like the house of Pharez, whom Tamar bare unto Judah, of the seed which the Lord shall give thee of this young woman.*

So Boaz took Ruth, and she was his wife: and when he went in unto her, the Lord gave her conception, and she bare a son. And the women said unto Naomi, Blessed be the Lord, which hath not left thee this day without a kinsman, that his name may be famous in Israel. And he shall be unto thee a restorer of thy life, and a nourisher of thine old age: for thy daughter in law, which loveth thee, which is better to thee than seven sons, hath born him. And Naomi took the child, and laid it in her bosom, and became nurse unto it. And the women her neighbours gave it a name, saying, There is a son born to Naomi; and they called his name Obed: he is the father of Jesse, the father of David. (Ruth 4:7-17)

We have seen how the nearest kinsman, as a type of the law, admitted his inability to redeem the inheritance. If a man breaks one of the Ten Commandments he is guilty of all. Now we have all sinned and broken God's law and we cannot, therefore, hope to be redeemed by the law. Paul, in chapter seven of the Book of Romans, shows in great detail the inability of the law to redeem a man: ". . . for what I would, that do I not; but what I hate, that do I" (v. 15). "Oh wretched man that I am!" he cries out; who shall deliver me, who shall redeem me, who shall buy me back? He concludes by saying, "I thank God through Jesus Christ our Lord" (vs. 24, 25).

Now we shall see how faithful Boaz, as a type of Christ, carried out the promise which he had made to Ruth and actually confirmed the transaction, taking her to be his wife and begetting a son of her. Remember that our Lord Jesus Christ, our greater Boaz, is faithful in the work which He has begun to do and He will surely perform it until the last day. What He has promised He is able also to perform. Adam, by his fall, by his doubt of the Word of God, brought sin into this world and death by sin, so that now all that are in Adam are estranged from God and have lost their inheritance in Him. But Christ has redeemed us and brought us back to God, restored us to fellowship with Him. Oh, that the Spirit of God and of grace would burn this truth into your mind and write it upon your heart! Christ alone, our Kinsman-Redeemer, is able to redeem us. Who shall deliver us? Not the church, not the creed, no organization, no effort that we can make. There is only One in heaven and in earth who can—the Lord Jesus Christ. He is our Boaz, our mighty Man of wealth, in whom we are possessed of all the riches of God. He became sin for us, tasted death on our behalf, in order that He might redeem us unto Himself, a people for His own possession.

A TESTIMONY IN ISRAEL

Looking more closely at the text, we note this strange custom whereby the shoe is plucked off as a testimony in Israel. The kinsman said, in effect, to Boaz, "Buy the ground for me. I cannot do it for myself." He then drew off his shoe. This was the custom in ancient times in Israel by which they symbolized and attested the truth that all rights of inheritance were given to another. So the nearest of kin drew off his shoe and handed it over to Boaz, thus transferring to him the legal right. Probably this custom symbolized the notion that Boaz, who received his kinsman's shoe, had the right to plant his own foot in the place of the nearer kinsman on the parcel of ground which had been left by Elimelech, and to claim it as his own for the house of Elimelech. With solemn emotion, Boaz then called the elders and all the bystanders to observe what had happened and to be witnesses to the legal fulness of what had been done. "You are witnesses this day," he says in effect, "that I have acquired all that belonged to Elimelech at the hand of Naomi, his wife; and that moreover Ruth, the wife of her son Mahlon, I am hereby taking to be my wife, that I may by her raise up the name of the dead upon his inheritance." All the people then replied solemnly, "We are witnesses." And so the legal transaction was finished.

We may well imagine that next there was a profusion of good wishes made to Boaz from all sides; and the writer of the history sums this up by saying that they invoked the blessing of God upon the marriage which was about to be consummated, to the end that Ruth might be a mother in Israel like Rachel and Leah had been. They lifted her up to the level of the very most famous women in their nation; and this would seem to indicate that the elders of Bethlehem concurred in the wisdom of Boaz' judgment, and did believe that Ruth, though she was an alien by birth, was indeed a true Israelite, an ornament to her husband-to-be for her love and her devotion to the God of Israel.

THE FULL REWARD OF FAITHFULNESS

Boaz having now removed all legal obstacles, takes Ruth to be his wife and in due time a son is born to them. And so Naomi and Ruth received the full reward of their faithfulness. Notice that the concluding part of our story is devoted primarily not to the young and happy mother and wife, but to the aged grandmother, Naomi, who had at the beginning of the book suffered so many calamities. It is to Naomi that attention is drawn, as the women who were her neighbors now congratulate her upon the birth of Ruth's son, and pray that as this boy comes to years he may restore to her, his grandmother, some of the former happiness and honor which she enjoyed in better days. Notice also what a fine tribute they pay to Ruth when they refer to her as the daughter-in-law who loves Naomi and is better to her than seven sons. Wherever was such a eulogy pronounced in all Israel upon a foreign woman? Wherever were such words ever found before on Hebrew lips? The story comes to a climax when we are told that Obed, Ruth's son, is the grandfather of David, the great king of Israel, who is himself the father and type of our Lord Jesus Christ. And so Ruth the Moabitess, Ruth the Gentile stranger, in the providence of God is brought into the direct line of Messiah, who in due course will rise from the ranks of her family to be the Light to lighten the Gentiles and the Glory of His people Israel. And thus we see how Ruth proved by her faithfulness the truth that ". . . all things work together for good to them that love God, to them who are the called according to his purpose" (Romans 8:28). For God did for her exceeding abundantly above all that she could ask or think; and He will do the same for you this very day if, like Ruth, you will come to the feet of the Lord Jesus, the Boaz of His people, the Redeemer of all those who seek Him.

OUR KINSMAN-REDEEMER

May I close our study of the little Book of Ruth by stressing once more the fact that we have in Boaz' redemption of Ruth and her inheritance a type of the redemption wrought for us by our divine Kinsman, the Lord Jesus Christ. This is the lesson I would leave with you. This is the truth I would above all others underline in your mind. Under the image and type of Boaz we have presented to us the all-important truth that, just as no poor Hebrew need suffer the loss of his land and his inheritance, so we do not need to suffer the loss of our souls because of our sins. Though we be enslaved to a hard taskmaster, Satan, though we be fallen into a bitter and shameful condition by our wickedness, Christ can and will redeem us from all iniquity if we will put our trust in Him. We cannot ourselves subdue our evil passions and lusts; we cannot regain the righteousness which we have lost and cast away. But there is One who is near of kin, who has become our Brother, who has taken upon Himself flesh like as we have, and has been made in all points like unto us, apart from sin, that He might confer on us the pardon of sin and bring us into the liberty of the sons of God. Oh, let us then exclaim with Naomi, "This Man is near of kin unto us! Blessed is He of the Lord, who hath not left off His kindness to the living and to the dead!" Let us this day, while it is today, come unto Him and confess our sins. Oh sinner, seek the Lord while He may be found; call ye upon Him while He is near. ". . . behold, now is the accepted time; behold, now is the day of salvation" (II Corinthians 6:2).